SimplyHealthful

FISH

THE SIMPLY HEALTHFUL SERIES

Simply Healthful Fish by David Ricketts and Susan McQuillan
Simply Healthful Pasta Salads by Andrea Chesman
Simply Healthful Cakes by Donna Deane and Minnie Bernardino

Simply Healthful

FISH

Delicious New Low-Fat Recipes

By David Ricketts & Susan McQuillan

Photography by Becky Luigart-Stayner

CHAPTERS PUBLISHING LTD., SHELBURNE, VERMONT 05482

Published by
Chapters Publishing Ltd.
2031 Shelburne Road
Shelburne, Vermont 05482

Library of Congress Cataloguing-in-Publication Data

Ricketts, David.
Simply healthful fish / by David Ricketts and Susan McQuillan:
photography by Becky Luigart-Stayner.
p. cm. -- (Simply healthful series)
Includes index.
ISBN 1-881527-05-0 : $9.95
1. Cookery (Fish) 2. Cookery (Shellfish)
I. McQuillan, Susan. II. Title III. Series.
TX747.R57 1993
641.6'92--dc20
92-39978
CIP

Trade distribution by
Firefly Books Ltd.
250 Sparks Avenue
Willowdale, Ontario
Canada M2H 2S4

Printed and bound in Canada by
Friesen Printers
Altona, Manitoba

Designed by Hans Teensma/Impress, Inc.

Contents

Introduction

THIRTY, twenty or even ten years ago, this book might not have been written. Back then, a wide variety of readily available fish would have been unheard of in Spencertown, the small rural village in Upstate New York where we prepared many of these recipes. But airplanes, refrigerated trucks, flash-freezing on shipboard and the science of aquaculture or fish farming have helped to bring fresh fish—from Long Island mako shark to farm-raised catfish from Florida—not only to Spencertown but to the tables in towns all over America.

Taking advantage of this bounty, we selected 16 commonly available fish and shellfish. The resulting recipes reveal the versatility of fish, incorporating a spectrum of cooking techniques and flavor combinations, some of which may surprise you. All are simple to prepare and are cooked with little or no added fat. For each recipe, we've listed other fish that can be substituted with equally excellent results.

Fresh fish fits naturally into a healthful eating plan because it's low in calories and fat, high in protein and a significant source of B vitamins and minerals, which are essential to health and muscle tone. Even the fat found in seafood is thought to be beneficial since it's rich in omega-3 fatty acids, components of polyunsaturated fats that are believed to play a preventive role in heart disease.

For the busy cook, the simplicity of preparing fish may be its best recommendation. A fish fillet or steak cooks quickly, in 4 to 12 minutes, because there is little connective tissue. Fatty fish such as mackerel, bluefish, salmon and tuna can be baked, broiled or grilled with little or no added fat, while leaner varieties such as flounder, sole, cod and halibut can be sautéed or broiled with just a little oil for flavor. For all types of fish, poaching and steaming are ideal low-fat cooking methods since they add no fat and keep the fish moist.

The generally mild and subtle flavor of fish lends itself to a wide range of flavorful preparations. In baking, broiling or sautéing, spices and fresh herbs or even jam-based glazes give bursts of flavor. Yogurt adds creaminess to some sauces without contributing excess fat, while honey lends subtle sweetness, and mustard or horseradish a sharper edge. Cooking fish with ingredients like tomato and kale, sugar snap peas and baby corn, or mango and mint, or serving it with a separate accompaniment such as fruit salsa, chutney, relish or a citrus sauce further enlivens the possibilities. Often, unexpected combinations of seasonings, such as jalapeño and ginger, or hot red pepper and pineapple, can play off one another, supplying simultaneous sensations of sweetness and heat.

Whatever cooking technique you use, remember one important caveat: Never overcook fish. It should be opaque in the center and just beginning to flake when prodded with a fork. Plan on 1¼ pounds of uncooked lean fish for 4 servings, or for a fattier fish such as mackerel, a pound will probably do.

If you're not already an enthusiast, the recipes that follow are likely to change your ideas about fish. If you're already a fish lover, these pages offer plenty of new ideas.

––––––––––

THE FOLLOWING GUIDELINES were used in determining the nutritional analysis of each recipe:

★ When a recipe offers a choice within the ingredient list, the first ingredient listed is the one represented in the nutritional analysis.

★ When an ingredient is listed as "optional," it is not included in the analysis.

Taking Care of the Catch

GONE ARE THE DAYS when we hesitated to cook fish because it smelled up the house and the family complained that dinner tasted fishy. Learn to spot truly fresh fish in the market, properly store and cook it, and your family will look forward to eating it.

Rely on your eyes and nose—they're your best guides for testing for freshness. Choose your fish source as carefully as you would select a new doctor—displays should sparkle and the fish should always look at its peak.

Avoid the purveyor who is reluctant to answer questions or who hesitates to give you a close look at the fish. If you have any problems at all with fish or shellfish when you get it home and unwrap it, take it back to the vendor without delay.

Buying and Storing Fresh Fish

★ Purchase fish displayed on ice in a refrigerated case in a reputable fish market or reliable supermarket. Avoid the unknown roadside fishmonger whose prices may be cheaper, but who may lack the equipment to chill the fish properly and who may be fishing illegally in contaminated waters.

★ When buying whole fish, check that the eyes are bright and clear and bulge a little, the scales are shiny and the gills behind the head are red.

★ The flesh of fillets, steaks and other cuts should be translucent, firm but springy to the touch (even through plastic wrap), unblemished, without any discoloration around the edges, and without tears.

★ Seafood should have a mild seaweedy or briny odor. If the fish is not easily accessible, don't be afraid to ask to take a sniff. Avoid fish that smells fishy or like ammonia—a sure sign that decay has set in.

★ Make your fish purchases at the end of your shopping trip, and take them home as soon as possible so you can refrigerate them.

★ Fish should not be refrigerated at home for more than 1 day. To store, rinse under cold running water, place in an airtight, nonabsorbent container and refrigerate at between 32 degrees F and 35 degrees F. Refrigerated fish should be cold to the touch, not cool.

★ If storing fresh fish for more than 1 day, freeze at 0 degrees F and use within 6 months.

Buying and Storing Frozen Fish

★ Use the same criteria for purchasing frozen fish as you would for any frozen food.

★ The package should be frozen solid and tightly wrapped, with no discoloration or ice crystals, which indicate previous thawing or partial thawing and then refreezing.

★ Do not purchase packages above the frost line in a store's freezer.

★ Store frozen fish at 0 degrees F for up to 6 months.

Thawing Frozen Fish

★ Place on a plate in the refrigerator overnight. A 1-pound package will thaw in about 24 hours. Do not thaw fish at room temperature or with hot or warm water.

★ To quick-thaw fish, defrost in original wrapper under cold running water.

★ To thaw frozen fish in a microwave oven, follow manufacturer's directions. Cook fish immediately after thawing.

Working With Fish

★ To guard against bacterial contamination, take the same precautions as you would with any raw animal product. Remember to wash hands, cutting boards, knives and anything else that comes in contact with the fish, with hot soapy water, before and after handling. Be sure to rinse thoroughly.

★ Be sure sponges or towels are clean before and after use.

★ Keep raw seafood away from cooked; they should not share the same plate.

★ Fish should not be kept unrefrigerated for more than 2 hours, including cooking time.

Cooking Fish

★ Rinse fish under cold running water to remove surface bacteria.

★ Be sure that all seafood is thoroughly cooked, all the way through, to a minimum internal temperature of 145 degrees F to kill any bacteria or parasites. Some restaurants prefer to serve tuna and other fish slightly underdone in the center. To be on the safe side, avoid this, whether eating at home or in a restaurant.

★ On the other hand, do not overcook fish, which will make it dry and, in some cases, tough. Cook just until opaque in the center and, for flaky fish, until fish begins to separate easily when touched with a fork.

★ The usual rule for cooking fish is 10 minutes per inch of thickness, regardless of method. This will vary according to oven accuracy or burner heat and initial temperature of fish.

★ When broiling or grilling, lightly brush rack with oil, rather than brushing it on fish.

Buying and Storing Live Shellfish

★ As with fresh fish, buy only from reliable, known sources, where the shellfish are properly displayed. Avoid shellfish with an ammonia or other "off" smell.

★ Shellfish that are purchased live, including clams, oysters, mussels, crabs and lobsters, should be just that—alive. Lobsters and crabs should move when prodded, and bivalves—mollusks with two shells, such as clams and mussels—must have unbroken shells that are tightly closed or at least close up when handled.

★ Refrigerate live shellfish in a well-ventilated container, covered with dampened paper toweling; shellfish need air and moisture.

★ Do not keep live shellfish for more than 1 day.

★ Keep fresh crabmeat refrigerated and use as soon as possible after purchase.

Working With Shellfish

★ Follow the caveats in "Working With Fish."

★ Scrub live clams, mussels and oysters with a stiff brush in clean water before shucking or cooking. Never submerge shellfish in water, other than for scrubbing. Unsalted water may upset the salt balance in the tissue and kill the shellfish.

★ The dark vein in shrimp is usually removed for aesthetic reasons. In large shrimp, it may in fact be gritty. To shell and devein shrimp: With kitchen shears or a small paring knife, cut through the shell along the outer curve and into the shrimp about $\frac{1}{16}$ inch to expose the vein. Peel back the shell from the cut and gently separate the shell, including the tail, from the shrimp. With the tip of a small knife, pull out the thin vein and discard.

What's in It for You

FISH (3 oz cooked)	CALORIES	FAT (g)	CHOLESTEROL (mg)
Bluefish	135	4	54
Catfish	120	5	60
Cod	90	1	50
Crab	90	1	80
Flounder	100	1	50
Sole	100	1	60
Halibut	120	2	30
Mackerel	220	15	60
Salmon	150	7	50
Scallops	95	1	45
Shark	120	3	50
Shrimp	85	2	160
Snapper	109	1	40
Swordfish	132	4	43
Trout	130	4	60
Tuna	163	6	43

Note: These are approximate figures.
Nutritional values may vary depending on species, origin and season.

Bluefish

NATIVE TO THE WATERS of the Atlantic, bluefish grow up to almost 4 feet in length and weigh as much as 32 pounds. This fish has a dark, soft-textured, full-flavored flesh that is best baked, broiled or grilled. Since the fish is oily, no extra fat is needed for cooking—an added benefit for low-fat cuisine. In addition, the natural oils present in these fish are high in omega-3 fatty acids, which are thought to lower blood cholesterol. When preparing the fillet, remove the darker strip of flesh running down the center as it may have a "fishy" flavor.

The rich flavor of bluefish takes well to assertive seasoning—in this case, a Middle Eastern influence. For a traditional touch, serve with corn on the cob, potato salad dressed with low-fat plain yogurt and a touch of mayonnaise, and a green salad.

Broiled Bluefish With Cumin

(also good with mackerel, salmon, tuna)

½	cup fresh lemon juice (from 2 lemons)
2	cloves garlic, crushed through a press
1	teaspoon cumin seeds
½	teaspoon ground coriander
½	teaspoon freshly grated nutmeg or ¼ teaspoon ground
1¼	pounds bluefish fillets

1. Combine lemon juice and garlic in glass or enamel dish just large enough to hold fish in single layer. Crush together cumin, coriander and nutmeg with a mortar and pestle. Add to lemon juice. Place fish in dish; turn to coat. Refrigerate, covered, turning fish over occasionally, for 30 to 60 minutes.

2. Preheat broiler. Remove fish from marinade. Pour marinade into small saucepan and boil for about 2 minutes.

3. Meanwhile, broil fish about 4 inches from heat for 4 to 6 minutes per side, depending on thickness of fillets or steaks, or until fish is opaque in center and begins to flake when touched with fork. Cut into 4 equal portions if necessary.

4. To serve, drizzle cooked marinade over fish.

Makes 4 servings.

189 CALORIES PER SERVING: 29 G PROTEIN; 6 G FAT; 4 G CARBOHYDRATE; 87 MG SODIUM; 83 MG CHOLESTEROL.

Broiled Bluefish With Horseradish and Apple

(also good with tuna, swordfish, shark)

1	tablespoon drained bottled horseradish, or more to taste
1	Granny Smith apple, peeled, cored and grated
1¼	pounds bluefish fillets

1. Preheat broiler. Combine horseradish and apple with a fork in small bowl. Spread half of apple mixture over one side of fillets.

2. Broil fish about 4 inches from heat for 4 to 6 minutes per side, spreading remaining apple mixture on second side. Cooking time will depend on thickness of fillets or steaks; cook until fish is opaque in center and begins to flake when touched with fork. Cut into 4 equal portions if necessary.

Makes 4 servings.

197 CALORIES PER SERVING: 28 G PROTEIN; 6 G FAT; 6 G CARBOHYDRATE; 127 MG SODIUM; 83 MG CHOLESTEROL.

The classic combination of apple and horseradish teams up well with full-flavored fishes. Some of the grated apple will darken when broiled, but this only adds to the flavor. Fill out the plate with boiled potatoes, mashed with a little yogurt, and steamed fresh peas.

Catfish

WHILE THERE ARE saltwater catfishes, the freshwater varieties are the ones commonly found in the markets. Most often farm-raised in freshwater ponds, they have firm, white flesh, with an almost sweet taste. Usually sold as fillets, catfish can be cooked by practically any method, the most well known being the "blackened" version popularized in New Orleans.

Catfish Stew
(see recipe, page 18)

*S*erve this light stew with crusty bread and a crisp cucumber salad. Substitute collard greens for the kale if you like, and add leftover cooked rice if you have some.

Catfish Stew

(also good with cod, scrod, orange roughy)

1	tablespoon olive oil
1	large onion, finely chopped or sliced
2	cloves garlic, finely chopped
1¼	pounds tomatoes, cored, seeded and chopped
1	package (10 ounces) frozen chopped kale, thawed
2	bottles (8 ounces each) clam juice or 1 can (14½ ounces) reduced-sodium chicken broth
1	tablespoon fresh thyme leaves or ¾ teaspoon dried
1¼	pounds catfish fillets, cut into 2-inch pieces
1	tablespoon fresh lemon juice
	Freshly ground black pepper to taste

1. Heat oil in large saucepot over medium heat. Add onion; sauté 3 minutes. Add garlic; sauté 1 minute. Add tomatoes, kale, clam juice or chicken stock, and thyme. Bring to boiling over medium-high heat. Lower heat; simmer 5 minutes.

2. Add catfish, lemon juice and pepper to taste. Cover and simmer 10 minutes, or until fish just flakes when touched with fork. Serve at once.

Makes 6 servings.

179 CALORIES PER SERVING: 20 G PROTEIN; 7 G FAT; 10 G CARBOHYDRATE; 249 MG SODIUM; 54 MG CHOLESTEROL.

Blackened Catfish

(also good with cod, tilapia, orange roughy, mackerel, bluefish)

YOGURT-SCALLION SAUCE
- ½ cup low-fat plain yogurt
- 2 tablespoons finely chopped scallion
- 1 teaspoon Dijon-style mustard
- 1 teaspoon lemon juice
- ⅛ teaspoon salt
- ⅛ teaspoon freshly ground black pepper

CAJUN SPICE
- 2 tablespoons paprika
- 2 teaspoons chili powder
- 1 teaspoon onion powder (optional)
- 1 teaspoon dried oregano
- 1 teaspoon dried marjoram
- ¾ teaspoon salt
- ½ teaspoon ground cumin
- ¼ teaspoon ground cinnamon
- ¼ teaspoon ground hot red pepper (cayenne)

CATFISH
- 1 pound catfish fillets in 4 pieces, about ¾ inch thick
- 1 teaspoon vegetable oil
- 1 lemon, cut into wedges

1. Prepare Sauce: Combine yogurt, scallion, mustard, lemon juice, salt and pepper in a small bowl. Refrigerate, covered, for up to 1 day before serving.

2. Heat well-seasoned cast-iron skillet or other heavy skillet over medium heat until very hot, about 5 minutes.

3. Meanwhile, combine paprika, chili powder, onion powder, if using, oregano, marjoram, salt, cumin, cinnamon and red pepper in shallow plate. Coat fish fillets on both sides with mixture.

Our version of the popular favorite that originated in New Orleans. The secret is in the skillet: It should be cast iron, well seasoned and preheated for 5 minutes before cooking the fish. Try this recipe once, then feel free to experiment with seasonings. Serve with a combination of black beans, corn and finely chopped tomato, or with steamed okra, stewed tomatoes and mashed potatoes.

(continued on page 20)

4. Add oil to skillet. Heat. Add fish to skillet. Cook 2 to 4 minutes on each side, depending on thickness of fish, turning once, or until fish is opaque in center and begins to flake when touched with fork. Serve with lemon wedges and Yogurt-Scallion Sauce.

Makes 4 servings.

181 CALORIES PER SERVING WITH SAUCE: 22 G PROTEIN; 8 G FAT; 6 G CARBOHYDRATE; 591 MG SODIUM; 67 MG CHOLESTEROL.

Cod

COD CAN BE FOUND on both coasts in North America and belongs to a large family that includes Atlantic cod, cusk, haddock, hake, Pacific and Atlantic tomcod and pollock. The Atlantic cod can grow up to 6 feet long and weigh up to almost 100 pounds. The flesh is lean, firm and white, and will flake easily when properly cooked. Highly versatile, the mild-tasting cod takes well to poaching, steaming, braising, stewing, baking, broiling, grilling and sautéing. "Scrod" is often used to describe young or small cod.

This Provençal-style sauce is even better if made a day or two ahead, but then omit the fresh herb and add it just before cooking. Try substituting fresh cilantro, oregano or flat-leaf Italian parsley for the basil. Serve with sliced baked sweet potatoes and steamed broccoli.

Baked Cod With Tomato and Black Olives

(also good with scrod, hake, haddock, halibut, tilefish, monkfish, grouper, snapper, sea bass, tilapia)

1	teaspoon vegetable oil
1	medium-size onion, chopped
2	cloves garlic, chopped
1	can (about 15 ounces) crushed tomatoes, packed in puree
¾	cup black olives, packed in water, drained, pitted and chopped
1	tablespoon grated lemon zest
¼	teaspoon salt
¼	teaspoon freshly ground black pepper
½	cup packed basil leaves or 1 tablespoon dried
1¼	pounds cod fillets
2	tablespoons sliced almonds, toasted

1. Heat oil in medium-size nonstick saucepan. Add onion; cook over low heat, covered, stirring occasionally, until softened, about 5 minutes. Add garlic; cook 30 seconds. Add tomatoes, olives, lemon zest, salt and pepper. Bring to boiling. Lower heat; simmer, uncovered, until thickened, about 20 minutes. Cut basil into thin strips; stir into sauce.

2. Preheat oven to 425 degrees F. Place fish in single layer in baking dish. Cover evenly with tomato sauce.

3. Bake for 15 to 20 minutes, depending on thickness of fish, or until fish is opaque in center and begins to flake when touched with fork. Cut into 4 equal portions if necessary.

4. To serve, garnish with toasted almonds.

Makes 4 servings.

214 CALORIES PER SERVING: 26 G PROTEIN; 9 G FAT; 10 G CARBOHYDRATE; 527 MG SODIUM; 56 MG CHOLESTEROL.

Broiled Cod With Sun-Dried Tomato Sauce

(also good with haddock, halibut, tilefish, grouper, snapper, tilapia, swordfish, tuna)

SUN-DRIED TOMATO SAUCE

½   cup water
½   cup dry-pack sun-dried tomatoes
2   teaspoons olive oil
1   medium-size onion, finely chopped
1   clove garlic, finely chopped
1   can (about 15 ounces) whole tomatoes, packed in juice
½   teaspoon freshly ground black pepper
1   tablespoon balsamic vinegar or red-wine vinegar

1¼   pounds cod fillets

1. Prepare Sauce: Bring water to boiling in small saucepan. Add sun-dried tomatoes. Boil 2 minutes or until softened. Drain, reserving liquid. Chop softened sun-dried tomatoes, removing any stems and discarding.

2. Heat oil in medium-size nonstick skillet. Add onion; cook, covered, over low heat, stirring occasionally, until softened, about 5 minutes. Add garlic; cook 30 seconds. Add sun-dried tomatoes with their liquid, canned tomatoes with their liquid, and pepper. Bring to boiling. Lower heat; simmer, stirring occasionally, until thickened, 20 to 30 minutes.

3. Stir in vinegar. Remove from heat. Preheat broiler.

4. Broil fish about 4 inches from heat for 4 to 6 minutes per side, depending on thickness, or until fish is opaque in center and begins to flake when touched with fork. Cut into 4 equal portions if necessary.

5. Serve the fish with the sauce warm or at room temperature.

Makes 4 servings (2 cups sauce).

156 CALORIES PER SERVING (WITH ¼ CUP SAUCE): 25 G PROTEIN; 2 G FAT; 9 G CARBOHYDRATE; 176 MG SODIUM; 56 MG CHOLESTEROL.

Adding sun-dried tomatoes to the ordinary canned variety brings a welcome intensity. To keep the dish low in fat, use dry-pack sun-dried tomatoes, not the ones packed in oil.

To save time, prepare the sauce up to three days ahead, without the addition of the vinegar, and refrigerate. To serve, gently reheat, add the vinegar and, for extra flavor, a handful of chopped fresh herbs, such as basil, mint, oregano or flat-leaf Italian parsley. The leftover chilled sauce is also delicious on chicken or grilled flank steak and even as a sandwich spread. Serve the fish with steamed new potatoes and your favorite green vegetable.

To soak up the citrusy sauce, serve the cod with rice (white or one of the many basmati-types now available), orzo, or for an Asian touch, cellophane noodles. Make the crisp ginger threads on their own and use to garnish poached chicken breasts, steamed or blanched vegetables, and even frozen yogurt or ice milk.

Cod With Orange-Ginger Sauce

(also good with scrod, hake, haddock, halibut, tilefish, grouper, mackerel, bluefish)

1	piece fresh ginger (2 x 1 inch), peeled
2	teaspoons vegetable oil
2	cups orange juice
1	tablespoon peeled, grated fresh ginger
1	tablespoon Dijon-style mustard
¼	teaspoon freshly ground black pepper
1¼	pounds cod fillets
	Scallion strips for garnish (optional)

1. Cut ginger lengthwise into thin slices. Stack slices; cut lengthwise into thin strips.

2. Heat oil in medium-size nonstick skillet. Add ginger strips; sauté until golden brown and crisp, about 3 minutes. Transfer to paper toweling to drain. Wipe out skillet.

3. Combine orange juice, grated ginger, mustard and pepper in skillet. Bring to boiling. Add fish in single layer. Return to boiling. Lower heat; cover and gently cook 6 to 10 minutes, depending on thickness of fish, or until fish is opaque in center and begins to flake when touched with fork. Remove fillets with slotted spoon to plate and keep warm. Cut into 4 equal portions if necessary.

4. Boil sauce over high heat until it reaches desired consistency, about 8 minutes for a thickened sauce.

5. To serve, spoon sauce over fillets. Garnish with crisp ginger threads and scallion strips, if using.

Makes 4 servings.

192 CALORIES PER SERVING: 25 G PROTEIN; 4 G FAT; 15 G CARBOHYDRATE; 133 MG SODIUM; 56 MG CHOLESTEROL.

Cod Chowder With Corn

(also good with scrod, hake, haddock, halibut, tilefish, monkfish, grouper, clams)

S*kim milk keeps the fat down in this red chowder, while the pureed potato contributes body. Plan to make the chowder a day ahead since the flavor will improve, and stir as little as possible to make sure the chunks of fish stay whole. Offer with crusty whole-wheat bread and a salad with a sharp-tasting green such, as arugula.*

1	tablespoon vegetable oil
2	thin slices Canadian bacon (about 1 ounce), chopped
1	medium-size onion, finely chopped
1	stalk celery, finely chopped
1	carrot, trimmed, peeled and finely chopped
1	pound tomatoes, cored, seeded and coarsely chopped
1	pound potatoes, scrubbed and cut into small dice
1	bottle (8 ounces) clam juice
1	quart skim milk
1	teaspoon dried rosemary
1	teaspoon dried oregano
½	teaspoon dried thyme
¼	teaspoon salt
¼	teaspoon freshly ground black pepper
2	cups fresh corn kernels or 1 package (10 ounces) frozen
1¼	pounds cod fillets, cut into chunks
	Chopped fresh dill or parsley for garnish
	Lemon wedges

1. Heat oil in medium-size nonstick pot. Add bacon; cook for 1 minute. Add onion; cover and cook, stirring occasionally, over low heat, 2 minutes. Add celery and carrot; cook, covered, stirring occasionally, until softened, about 10 minutes. Add tomatoes; cook until softened, about 3 minutes.

2. Add potatoes, clam juice and milk. Bring to gentle boil. Lower heat; simmer, covered, until potato is tender, 8 to 10 minutes.

3. Drain soup in colander over a large bowl. Working in batches, puree solids in food processor or blender, adding a little liquid with each batch. Whisk puree into drained liquid.

4. Add rosemary, oregano, thyme, salt and pepper to chowder. Add corn and fish. Gently simmer until cod is cooked through, about 10 minutes. Serve, or cool and refrigerate overnight. Gently reheat over very low heat to serve. Garnish each serving with the dill or parsley, and squeeze a little lemon into each.

Makes 8 servings (12 cups).

229 CALORIES PER SERVING: 20 G PROTEIN; 3 G FAT; 32 G CARBOHYDRATE; 309 MG SODIUM; 32 MG CHOLESTEROL.

Crab

A VARIETY OF CRABS inhabit the waters off both coasts. Hard-shell crabs, such as Dungeness and stone crab, are delicious when steamed or boiled, while the soft-shell variety is best lightly floured and quickly sautéed. If purchasing cooked crabmeat, remember that the choicest grade is lump or backfin: lump is big chunks of body meat, while backfin consists of smaller chunks.

Broiled Crab Cakes With Honey-Horseradish Sauce

(also good with leftover cooked cod or other flaky white fish)

HONEY-HORSERADISH SAUCE
½	cup low-fat plain yogurt
1	tablespoon honey
1	tablespoon Dijon-style mustard
1	teaspoon drained bottled horseradish

CRAB CAKES
2	egg whites
2	tablespoons Dijon-style mustard
1	tablespoon reduced-calorie mayonnaise
1	tablespoon fresh lemon juice
½	teaspoon salt
¼	teaspoon freshly ground black pepper
⅛	teaspoon ground hot red pepper (cayenne)
10	fat-free saltine crackers, finely crushed (½ cup)
2	tablespoons chopped fresh parsley
1	pound lump or backfin crabmeat

Chopped red bell pepper for garnish (optional)

1. Prepare Sauce: Combine yogurt, honey, mustard and horseradish in small bowl. Cover and refrigerate up to 2 days.

2. Prepare Crab Cakes: Lightly beat together egg whites, mustard, mayonnaise, lemon juice, salt, black pepper and red pepper in medium-size bowl. Stir in crackers and parsley until well mixed. Gently fold in crabmeat.

3. Gently shape mixture into 8 equal patties, about 3 inches in diameter and 1 inch thick. Place on lightly greased broiler pan. Refrigerate at least 1 hour or up to 4 hours before broiling.

We like our crab cakes plain and simple and very crabby, but some might add a dash of Worcestershire, a spoonful of grated fresh horseradish or a pinch or two of Old Bay seasoning. Broiling rather than frying eliminates the need for extra fat.

(continued on page 32)

4. Preheat broiler. Broil about 6 inches from heat for 5 minutes, or until cakes are browned on top and heated through to center. Carefully transfer to plates. Spoon 1 tablespoon sauce over each cake. Garnish with chopped sweet red pepper, if using. Serve at once.

Makes 8 cakes (8 appetizer servings or 4 main-course servings).

166 CALORIES PER MAIN-COURSE SERVING (WITH 1 TABLESPOON SAUCE): 24 G PROTEIN; 3 G FAT; 11 G CARBOHYDRATE; 848 MG SODIUM; 68 MG CHOLESTEROL.

Pasta Paolo

(also good with scallops, shrimp, lobster meat)

¾	pound radiatore, rotelle or small shell pasta
12	ounces arugula, well rinsed, or broccoli raab, Swiss chard or kale
1	tablespoon vegetable or olive oil
1	large onion, finely chopped
2	cloves garlic, finely chopped
3	pounds ripe plum tomatoes, cored, seeded and finely chopped
¼	cup dry white wine
½	teaspoon salt
¼	teaspoon freshly ground black pepper
¼	teaspoon crushed red pepper flakes
1	tablespoon fresh lemon juice
1	pound lump or backfin crabmeat

1. Cook pasta according to package directions until tender but somewhat firm to the bite. Drain.

2. Meanwhile, cook arugula, broccoli raab, Swiss chard or kale — with rinse water clinging to the leaves — in large skillet, covered, for 1 minute, or just until wilted. Drain and set aside. Dry skillet.

3. Heat oil in same skillet over medium heat. Add onion; sauté 3 minutes. Add garlic; sauté 1 minute. Add tomatoes, wine, salt, black pepper and pepper flakes. Simmer, stirring frequently, for 5 minutes, or until tomatoes are softened.

4. Stir greens and lemon juice into skillet. Gently stir in crabmeat. Simmer 1 minute, or until crab is heated through. Serve over hot cooked pasta.

Makes 6 servings.

393 CALORIES PER SERVING: 25 G PROTEIN; 5 G FAT; 62 G CARBOHYDRATE; 460 MG SODIUM; 45 MG CHOLESTEROL.

This simple summer dish, inspired by a recipe from Paolo Campanelli, a favored Italian hair stylist in New York City, stretches a pound of precious crabmeat into pasta sauce for six. The pepperiness of the arugula contrasts nicely with the sweetness of the crab and the tomato. Serve with a crisp green salad, a loaf of semolina bread and the remaining white wine not used in the dish.

Flounder

THESE BOTTOM-DWELLING flat-bodied fishes have eyes that are paired on the same side of the head, and swim with their blind side down. The many varieties include not only different types of flounder but also halibut, turbot and some soles. The boneless fillets are mild-flavored and lean, with a delicate texture, and are especially suited for poaching, sautéing and steaming.

Broiled Whole Flounder With Dry Fennel Marinade

(also good with sole, butterfish, porgy)

1 tablespoon fennel seeds, crushed
2 teaspoons grated lemon zest
1 teaspoon dried leaf thyme
1 teaspoon vegetable oil
½ teaspoon salt
2 whole flounders (1½–2 pounds each), cleaned, or 1¼ pounds
   flounder fillets

1. Combine fennel, lemon zest, thyme, oil and salt in small cup. Cut 3 diagonal slashes on top surface of fish. Rub fennel mixture over fish and into cuts. Cover and refrigerate for 2 to 4 hours.

2. Preheat broiler. Broil fish on lightly greased broiler pan about 6 inches from heat for 8 to 12 minutes, depending on thickness of fillets, or until fish is opaque in center and begins to flake when touched with fork. Divide into 4 equal portions. Serve at once.

Makes 4 servings.

146 CALORIES PER SERVING: 27 G PROTEIN; 3 G FAT; 1 G CARBOHYDRATE; 384 MG SODIUM; 75 MG CHOLESTEROL.

The sweet, tender white meat of the flounder is nicely set off by the delicate anise, or licorice-like, flavor of the fennel. Each whole flounder serves two people so you can easily halve, double or quadruple the recipe. Try this classic seasoning mixture with any fish, in any form.

No messy cleanup here, since fish fillets and vegetables steam together in individual foil packets. Serve straight from the packet, with rice or tiny steamed new potatoes, and herbed green beans on the side.

Oven-Steamed Flounder in Foil With Vegetables

(also good with sole, cod, mackerel, snapper, bluefish)

2	medium-size carrots, trimmed, peeled and cut into 2 x ¼-inch sticks
2	small stalks celery, cut into 2 x ¼-inch sticks
1	teaspoon vegetable oil
1	tablespoon fresh thyme leaves or 1 teaspoon dried
½	teaspoon salt
¼	teaspoon freshly ground black pepper
1¼	pounds flounder fillets
¼	cup dry vermouth
8	thin lemon slices

1. Cut four 18 x 12-inch rectangles from heavy-duty aluminum foil. Preheat oven to 400 degrees F with baking sheet in oven.

2. Toss carrots, celery, oil, 1½ teaspoons fresh thyme (½ teaspoon dried), ¼ teaspoon salt and ⅛ teaspoon pepper in medium-size bowl. Divide mixture evenly among foil rectangles, placing in center.

3. Lay fillets over vegetables, dividing equally and cutting them to fit, if necessary. Sprinkle evenly with vermouth and remaining thyme, salt and pepper. Lay 2 lemon slices on top of each fillet. Bring 2 long sides of foil up and over fish; fold edges over together twice. Fold short ends over twice to form tightly sealed packets.

4. Place foil packets on preheated baking sheet. Bake for 25 to 30 minutes, or until fish is opaque and vegetables are tender. To check for doneness, carefully unwrap one packet.

5. To serve, carefully cut open each packet and place on plate, or let each diner open his or her own.

Makes 4 servings.

175 CALORIES PER SERVING: 27 G PROTEIN; 3 G FAT; 5 G CARBOHYDRATE; 413 MG SODIUM; 75 MG CHOLESTEROL.

Baked Stuffed Flounder

(also good with sole)

2   teaspoons vegetable or olive oil
1   medium-size onion, finely chopped
1   clove garlic, finely chopped
½   cup fresh multi-grain bread crumbs (1 slice bread)
2   tablespoons chopped fresh parsley
2   teaspoons lemon juice
½   teaspoon dried marjoram
½   teaspoon salt
4   flounder fillets (about 5 ounces each)
¼   cup dry white wine or reduced-sodium chicken broth
        or clam juice
¼   teaspoon paprika (optional)

1. Preheat oven to 400 degrees F. Heat oil in small nonstick skillet over medium heat. Add onion and garlic: sauté 3 minutes, or until softened. Remove from heat. Stir in bread crumbs, parsley, lemon juice, marjoram and ¼ teaspoon salt.

2. Spread stuffing along the length of each fillet, dividing evenly. Roll up fillets; secure each with wooden pick. Place in glass pie plate or shallow baking dish. Add wine, chicken stock or clam juice. Sprinkle fillets with paprika, if using, and remaining ¼ teaspoon salt.

3. Bake, basting fish occasionally with pan liquids, for 20 minutes, or until fish begins to flake when touched with fork and stuffing is heated through. Remove wooden picks.

Makes 4 servings.

190 CALORIES PER SERVING: 28 G PROTEIN; 4 G FAT; 7 G CARBOHYDRATE; 429 MG SODIUM; 75 MG CHOLESTEROL.

Serve these marjoram-bread-crumb-stuffed flounder rolls alongside grilled or steamed zucchini with a fresh tomato salad on the side.

Flounder Fillets in Tomato-Ginger Sauce

(also good with sole, cod, tilapia)

2	teaspoons vegetable oil
1	large onion, finely chopped
2	cloves garlic, finely chopped
1	pound ripe tomatoes, cored, seeded and diced
¼	cup orange juice
1	tablespoon reduced-sodium soy sauce
1	tablespoon peeled, grated fresh ginger
¼	teaspoon salt
⅛	teaspoon freshly ground black pepper
1¼	pounds flounder fillets

1. Preheat oven to 375 degrees F. Heat oil in large nonstick skillet over medium heat. Add onion; sauté 3 minutes. Add garlic; sauté 1 minute. Stir in tomatoes, orange juice, soy sauce, ginger, salt and pepper. Bring to boiling. Lower heat; simmer 10 minutes, stirring occasionally.

2. Spoon ½ cup sauce into shallow baking dish or pie plate. Arrange fillets, overlapping, on top of sauce. Spoon remaining sauce over fillets.

3. Bake for 8 to 10 minutes, depending on thickness of fish, or until fish is opaque in center and begins to flake when touched with fork. Cut into 4 equal portions if necessary.

Makes 4 servings.

207 CALORIES PER SERVING: 28 G PROTEIN; 5 G FAT; 13 G CARBOHYDRATE; 387 MG SODIUM; 75 MG CHOLESTEROL.

Mustard-Crusted Flounder Fillets

(also good with cod, sole, turbot, pollock)

1¼	pounds flounder fillets
3	tablespoons low-fat plain yogurt
2	tablespoons finely chopped scallion
1	tablespoon Dijon-style mustard
1	tablespoon finely chopped fresh dill or 1 teaspoon dried
1	teaspoon fresh lemon juice
	Freshly ground black pepper to taste

1. Preheat broiler. Arrange fillets in single layer on lightly greased broiler pan. Combine yogurt, scallion, mustard, dill and lemon juice in small bowl. Spread evenly over fillets. Sprinkle with pepper to taste.

2. Broil fish about 4 inches from heat, without turning, for 4 to 6 minutes, depending on thickness of fillets, or until fish is opaque in center and begins to flake when touched with fork.

Makes 4 servings.

157 CALORIES PER SERVING: 31 G PROTEIN; 2 G FAT; I G CARBOHYDRATE; 190 MG SODIUM; 85 MG CHOLESTEROL.

Try different flavored mustards for slight variations. Serve with steamed Brussels sprouts, broccoli or cauliflower and slices of caraway rye bread.

The fillets are spread with a mustard-herb mixture, rolled up, and then braised in a light wine sauce. Serve with a wild and white rice combination and sliced tomatoes sprinkled with balsamic vinegar.

Flounder With Herb-Wine Sauce

(also good with sole, tilapia, cod, orange roughy)

4	flounder fillets (about 5 ounces each)
1	tablespoon Dijon-style mustard
2	teaspoons fresh marjoram leaves or 1 teaspoon dried
1	teaspoon fresh thyme leaves or ½ teaspoon dried
2	teaspoons olive oil
1	medium-size onion, finely chopped
1	stalk celery, finely chopped
2	cloves garlic, finely chopped
¼	teaspoon salt
⅛	teaspoon freshly ground black pepper
½	cup dry white wine
	Lemon wedges and fresh marjoram or thyme for garnish (optional)

1. Halve flounder fillets lengthwise to make 8 pieces. Combine mustard, 1 teaspoon marjoram (½ teaspoon dried) and ½ teaspoon thyme (¼ teaspoon dried) in small cup. Spread lightly and evenly on one side of fish pieces. Roll up fillets and secure with wooden pick.

2. Heat oil in large nonstick skillet over medium heat. Add onion; sauté 3 minutes. Add celery, garlic, remaining marjoram, remaining thyme, salt and pepper; sauté 2 minutes. Place fish rolls on top of vegetables. Pour wine over. Cover and simmer over low heat for 8 minutes, or until fish is opaque in center and begins to flake when touched with fork.

3. Remove fish rolls to serving plate; cover and keep warm. Puree skillet mixture in blender or small food processor until smooth.

4. To serve, remove wooden picks and pour sauce over fish rolls. Garnish with lemon wedges and sprigs of fresh herbs, if you wish.

Makes 4 servings.

205 CALORIES PER SERVING: 31 G PROTEIN; 5 G FAT; 4 G CARBOHYDRATE; 326 MG SODIUM; 84 MG CHOLESTEROL.

Halibut

ACTUALLY PART of the flounder family, halibut inhabits both the Pacific and Atlantic oceans. Two of the most popular varieties are Pacific and California halibut. Since halibut can measure up to 8 feet in length and weigh as much as 800 pounds, it is usually sold as steaks, unlike flounder, which is generally purchased as fillets. Halibut's firm, sweet flesh takes well to poaching, baking, sautéing, broiling and grilling, especially in kebabs.

Grilled Thai-Style Halibut Steaks

(also good with cod, shark, salmon)

2	tablespoons finely chopped, seeded jalapeño pepper (1–2 jalapeños)
1	tablespoon peeled, grated fresh ginger
2	cloves garlic, finely chopped
1	teaspoon grated lime zest
2	teaspoons fresh lime juice
¼	teaspoon salt
1¼	pounds halibut steaks

1. Preheat grill or broiler. Combine jalapeño, ginger, garlic, lime zest, lime juice and salt in small bowl. Crush slightly with fork to form paste. Rub mixture on both sides of fish steaks.

2. Grill or broil steaks about 4 inches from heat for 3 to 4 minutes on each side, turning once, depending on thickness of fish, or until fish is opaque in center and begins to flake when touched with fork. Cut into 4 equal portions if necessary.

Makes 4 servings.

161 CALORIES PER SERVING: 30 G PROTEIN; 3 G FAT; 1 G CARBOHYDRATE; 211 MG SODIUM; 46 MG CHOLESTEROL.

This one-dish meal contains a deliciously surprising combination of sweet, hot and tangy flavors. Serve with tortilla chips on the side, if you like, and finish the meal with a tangy-sweet citrus sorbet. You can spoon the corn mixture, hot or cold, over just about any fish.
(See photograph on the front cover.)

Mexicali Halibut

(also good with cod, scrod, turbot, tilapia)

1	tablespoon fresh lemon juice or lime juice
2	teaspoons vegetable oil
½	teaspoon ground cumin
¼	teaspoon ground cinnamon
¼	teaspoon salt
1¼	pounds halibut fillet in 1 piece or steaks
½	pound zucchini, trimmed and finely chopped
2	cups fresh corn kernels or 1 package (10 ounces) frozen corn kernels, thawed
1	can (14½ ounces) Mexican-style stewed tomatoes

1. Combine lemon or lime juice, 1 teaspoon oil, cumin, cinnamon and salt in small cup. Place fish on lightly greased broiler pan, tucking under thin end of fillet, if necessary, to ensure more even cooking. Brush with half the lemon mixture. Set aside for 15 minutes. Preheat broiler.

2. Meanwhile, heat remaining 1 teaspoon oil in medium-size non-stick skillet over medium heat. Add zucchini; sauté 3 minutes. Add corn and tomatoes. Bring to boiling over medium-high heat. Simmer rapidly for 5 minutes, without stirring, until most of the liquid cooks off. Cover and set aside.

3. Broil fish about 4 inches from heat, basting once or twice with remaining lemon mixture, for 8 minutes, or until fish is opaque in center and begins to flake when touched with a fork. Cut into 4 equal portions. Spoon corn mixture over fish to serve.

Makes 4 servings.

256 CALORIES PER SERVING: 33 G PROTEIN; 6 G FAT; 20 G CARBOHYDRATE; 494 MG SODIUM; 46 MG CHOLESTEROL.

Mackerel

TWENTY-THREE SPECIES of mackerel are found in North American waters and are part of the large family that includes bonito, tuna and albacore. Ranging in length from 1 to 1½ feet and weighing an average of 1 to 2 pounds, mackerel has an outer layer of oily muscle with less fatty interior meat. Freshness is crucial to capturing the distinctive mild mackerel flavor. Soft-fleshed, the fillets can be braised, stewed, baked, broiled, grilled or sautéed.

Baked Honey-Glazed Mackerel

(also good with bluefish, trout, tuna, swordfish, salmon, shark)

½	cup honey
2	tablespoons water
½	teaspoon ground allspice
½	teaspoon ground cloves
¼	teaspoon ground hot red pepper (cayenne)
1¼	pounds mackerel fillets

1. Preheat oven to 425 degrees F. Combine honey, water, allspice, cloves and red pepper in small bowl. Place fish in baking dish. Spread evenly with honey mixture.

2. Bake for 8 to 12 minutes, depending on thickness of fillets or steaks, or until fish is opaque in center and begins to flake when touched with fork. Cut into 4 equal portions if necessary.

Makes 4 servings.

424 CALORIES PER SERVING: 27 G PROTEIN; 20 G FAT; 34 G CARBOHYDRATE; 97 MG SODIUM; 84 MG CHOLESTEROL.

The flavor influence is Greek—sweet spices and honey, sharpened with a little hot red pepper. Serve with steamed carrots and zucchini, and orzo or rice seasoned with ground cumin.

The key to this recipe is slicing the lemon paper-thin, so the rind will soften as it cooks. Take your time to do the slicing properly. Mackerel is a fatty fish, so judiciously select side dishes low in fat, such as orzo and steamed zucchini rounds seasoned with a sprinkle of rosemary, or roasted onions.

Baked Mackerel With Lemon and Capers

(also good with bluefish, tuna, swordfish, salmon, monkfish, tilefish, tilapia, shark)

1¼	pounds mackerel fillets
¼	teaspoon freshly ground black pepper
1	lemon with rind, very thinly sliced and seeded
¼	cup capers, drained and rinsed

1. Preheat oven to 425 degrees F. Place fish in single layer in baking dish. Season with pepper. Cover evenly with lemon slices, then capers.

2. Bake for 8 to 12 minutes, depending on thickness of fillets or steaks, or until fish is opaque in center and begins to flake when touched with fork. Cut into 4 equal portions if necessary.

Makes 4 servings.

300 CALORIES PER SERVING: 27 G PROTEIN; 20 G FAT; 3 G CARBOHYDRATE; 269 MG SODIUM; 84 MG CHOLESTEROL.

Salmon

SALMON IS A MEMBER of the family that includes trout. The most common varieties are coho, sockeye and chinook from the Pacific coast, and the Atlantic salmon, but due to dwindling numbers in the wild, much of the salmon consumed in America is farm-raised, both in North America and overseas. Sold whole, in steaks or in fillets, the fish is firm-textured, fatty and full-flavored, with a somewhat sweet overtone. Salmon can be baked, grilled, broiled, poached or steamed.

Balsamic Salmon With Tarragon and Sweet Peppers

(also good with halibut, sea bass)

¼	cup orange juice
2	tablespoons balsamic vinegar or red-wine vinegar
1	tablespoon fresh tarragon leaves or 1 teaspoon dried
¾	teaspoon salt
⅛	teaspoon freshly ground black pepper
1½	pounds salmon fillet, in 1 piece
2	teaspoons vegetable oil
1	large onion, halved and thinly sliced
1	each sweet red, yellow and green bell peppers, cored, seeded and cut lengthwise into ¼-inch-wide strips
2	cloves garlic, finely chopped

1. Combine orange juice, vinegar, tarragon, ¼ teaspoon salt and pepper in large bowl. Add salmon fillet, turning to coat. Refrigerate, covered, for 30 minutes to 1 hour, turning occasionally.

2. Preheat broiler. Transfer salmon to broiler pan. Set aside ¼ cup of marinade; use remainder to baste fish.

3. Broil fish about 4 inches from heat for 3 to 5 minutes on each side, depending on thickness of fish, or until salmon is opaque in center, basting with marinade as you turn.

4. Meanwhile, heat oil in large nonstick skillet over medium-high heat. Add onion and peppers; sauté 3 minutes. Add garlic; sauté 1 minute longer. Add reserved ¼ cup marinade and remaining ½ teaspoon salt. Cook, stirring occasionally, until liquid almost evaporates.

5. To serve, cut salmon into 6 equal portions. Spoon onions and peppers over top.

Makes 6 servings.

149 CALORIES PER SERVING: 17 G PROTEIN; 5 G FAT; 7 G CARBOHYDRATE; 961 MG SODIUM; 20 MG CHOLESTEROL.

The balsamic vinegar adds a pungent note to the sweetness of the peppers and the richness of the salmon. For even cooking, start out with a fillet of uniform thickness. Hot cooked rice, wild or white, and a crisp green salad are all you need to round out the meal.
(See photograph on the back cover.)

Salmon Pâté

(also good with fresh and smoked trout)

1	pound fresh salmon fillet
1	pound low-fat (1 percent) cottage cheese
4	ounces Neufchâtel or "light" cream cheese
3	tablespoons bottled horseradish, drained
1	tablespoon fresh lemon juice
1	tablespoon Dijon-style mustard
4	ounces smoked salmon
1–2	tablespoons chopped fresh dill (optional)

1. Poach Salmon: Follow recipe for Citrus-Poached Salmon (page 62), substituting 1 sliced lemon for all the citrus. Or simply cover salmon with cold water in skillet or saucepan. Bring to boiling over medium-high heat. Lower heat; simmer 8 minutes, or just until salmon is opaque in center. Cool slightly in poaching liquid. Cool completely before using in pâté.

2. Process cottage cheese in food processor until very smooth, 1 to 2 minutes. Add Neufchâtel, horseradish, lemon juice and mustard. Pulse until blended. Break up poached fresh salmon and smoked salmon; add to processor. Process until mixture is smooth. Add dill, if using. Process until blended.

3. Scrape mixture into 4 cup crock or into smaller crocks. Cover and refrigerate at least overnight, or for up to 3 days before serving.

Makes 4 cups.

18 CALORIES PER TABLESPOON: 2 G PROTEIN; 1 G FAT; 0 G CARBOHYDRATE; 107 MG SODIUM; 3 MG CHOLESTEROL.

P*ureed cottage cheese serves as the base for this reduced-fat version of a classic spread. Using smoked salmon in addition to fresh gives depth of flavor to the pâté. This recipe is easily halved for a smaller crowd. Garnish with sprigs of fresh dill, thinly sliced red onion, and a few capers, if you like. Serve with water crackers, cucumber rounds, toast and celery sticks.*

Cooked salsa can be prepared up to a week ahead. Spoon it on hamburgers and grilled or broiled chicken, as well as on any fish. The drained relish juice doubles as a basting liquid. If green tomatoes are unavailable, substitute underripe red tomatoes or tomatillos, and to vary the citrus flavor, substitute grapefruit or lemon juice for the lime. Serve with three-bean salad and corn on the cob.

Grilled Salmon With Green Tomato-Chili Relish

(also good with shark, swordfish, halibut)

GREEN TOMATO-CHILI RELISH

1	pound green tomatoes, cored and finely chopped
1	cucumber, pared, seeded and finely chopped
2	scallions, trimmed and finely chopped
¼	cup finely chopped green bell pepper
1	clove garlic, finely chopped
1	jalapeño pepper, seeded and finely chopped
2	teaspoons sugar
¼	teaspoon salt
1	tablespoon fresh lime juice
1	tablespoon finely chopped fresh cilantro

6 salmon steaks (4–5 ounces each)

1. Prepare Relish: Combine tomatoes, cucumber, scallions, green pepper, garlic, jalapeño pepper, sugar and salt in nonaluminum medium-size skillet. Bring to simmering over medium heat; simmer 5 minutes. Remove from heat. Stir in lime juice. Cool completely. Refrigerate, covered, until ready to use, up to 1 week. To serve, drain relish, reserving liquid to use as a baste for poultry or other fish. Stir cilantro into relish just before serving.

2. Preheat grill or broiler. Grill or broil salmon about 4 inches from heat, basting often with reserved relish liquid, for 4 to 6 minutes per side, depending on thickness of steaks, or just until opaque in center and beginning to flake when touched with fork. Serve with chilled relish.

Makes 6 servings (about 2½ cups relish).

121 CALORIES PER SERVING (WITH ¼ CUP RELISH): 17 G PROTEIN; 4 G FAT; 4 G CARBOHYDRATE; 753 MG SODIUM; 20 MG CHOLESTEROL.

C hilled, sliced salmon is served on a bed of peppery watercress and drizzled with a fruity sauce that is sweetened with honey and sharpened with Dijon mustard. Prepare fish and sauce a day ahead and assemble the dish just before serving. Serve chilled as a first course or as the main course.

Citrus-Poached Salmon With Orange-Mustard Sauce

(also good with bass, halibut, tilefish, shark)

ORANGE-MUSTARD SAUCE
1	tablespoon Dijon-style mustard
1	tablespoon fresh lemon juice
2	teaspoons cornstarch
1	tablespoon honey
1	cup orange juice

SALMON
1¼	pounds salmon fillet, in 1 piece
1	cup dry white wine
½	cup water
1	orange, thinly sliced
1	lemon, thinly sliced
1	lime, thinly sliced
6	whole cloves
½	teaspoon salt
1	bunch watercress

1. Prepare Sauce: Stir together mustard, lemon juice, cornstarch and honey in small saucepan. Slowly stir in orange juice until well blended. Bring to boiling over medium heat, stirring slowly and constantly. Boil gently for 1 minute. Cool completely. Refrigerate, covered, until ready to serve.

2. Prepare Salmon: Place salmon in skillet just large enough to hold fillet without folding. Add wine, water, orange, lemon, lime, cloves and salt; if necessary, add more water or wine to cover fish completely.

3. Bring to gentle boil over medium-high heat. Lower heat; simmer 8 to 12 minutes, depending on thickness of fish, or until salmon is opaque in center. Remove salmon and citrus slices with slotted spatula. Wrap and refrigerate until ready to serve.

(continued on page 64)

4. To serve, arrange watercress on platter. Slice salmon and arrange on top of watercress. Drizzle with some Orange-Mustard Sauce. Serve remaining sauce on side.

Makes 6 first-course servings or 4 main-dish servings.

163 CALORIES PER MAIN-DISH SERVING (WITH 1 TABLESPOON SAUCE): 21 G PROTEIN; 3 G FAT; 4 G CARBOHYDRATE; 1123 MG SODIUM; 25 MG CHOLESTEROL.

Scallops

BELONGING TO A HUGE FAMILY with more than 400 members, the scallop is a bivalve mollusk with a sweet, mild flavor. Bay and calico are the smaller varieties; the deep-sea scallop is larger. So-called wet-pack scallops, whether fresh or frozen, are treated with polyphosphates to help retain moisture and prolong shelf life, and will usually shrink when cooked. Dry-pack scallops may appear smaller, but are moved through the processing chain more quickly, so in fact may be fresher. The scallop benefits most from a quick steaming, sautéing or poaching—overcooking yields a tough, rubbery texture.

The inspiration for this dish, in which pasta and scallops are cooked together in a packet, comes from Tony Cerny at his restaurant Casanova's in Pleasanton, California. Our version replaces the original parchment paper with heavy-duty aluminum foil. The packets can be prepared an hour or two ahead of time, refrigerated, then arranged on the preheated baking sheet in the oven for no-mess, no-effort cooking. The pasta can be cooked a day ahead and refrigerated.

Linguine and Scallops in Packets

(also good with cod, halibut, scrod, haddock, shrimp, mussels, lobster)

¾	pound linguine
2	tomatoes, cored, seeded and chopped (about 2 cups)
4	tablespoons finely chopped scallion
¼	cup chopped fresh basil or 2 teaspoons dried
¼	teaspoon salt
¼	teaspoon freshly ground black pepper
¾	pound sea scallops
¼	cup bottled clam broth or dry white wine
¼	cup grated Parmesan (optional)

1. Cook pasta according to package directions just until al dente, firm but slightly tender to the bite. Drain in a colander; rinse under cold running water to stop the cooking.

2. Preheat oven to 400 degrees F with baking sheet in oven.

3. Tear off 4 sheets of heavy-duty aluminum foil, 18 x 12 inches. Assemble each packet by arranging ingredients in the center of each sheet of foil in the following order: ¼ of the cooked pasta; ½ cup chopped tomato; 1 tablespoon scallion; 1 tablespoon chopped fresh basil or ½ teaspoon dried; pinch salt and pepper; ¼ of the scallops. Drizzle with 1 tablespoon clam broth or wine.

4. To seal each packet, bring 2 long sides of foil up and over fish; fold edges over together twice. Fold short ends over twice.

5. Place packets on preheated baking sheet. Bake for about 10 minutes. If packets have been refrigerated, allow about 2 extra minutes baking time.

6. To serve, allow diners to open their own packets. The pasta and scallops with sauce can be transferred to the plate. Each serving can be topped with 1 tablespoon grated Parmesan, if desired.

Makes 4 servings.

428 CALORIES PER SERVING: 26 G PROTEIN; 2 G FAT; 73 G CARBOHYDRATE; 312 MG SODIUM; 28 MG CHOLESTEROL.

Shark

SINCE SHARK HAS BECOME an increasingly popular food fish, some organizations are suggesting quotas for certain species. Of the many varieties of sharks that inhabit the Pacific and Atlantic waters, those available in the market include thresher, soupfin, leopard, Pacific angel and mako, considered by most to have the best flavor. Available in fillet or steak form, the firm-fleshed fish tastes similar to swordfish but not as sweet. Shark can be prepared using any of the cooking methods suitable for lean fish, such as grilling, broiling, steaming and poaching.

Grill fish steaks over medium-hot coals, or broil indoors, and serve with basmati rice flecked with chopped scallion, and a mixed green salad. You can refrigerate the leftover tomato chutney for up to 1 month to have on hand for spooning over hamburgers, chicken, pork or other cooked meats. The chutney's hot-sweet taste adds lively flavor without fat.

Shark Steaks With Tomato Chutney

(also good with swordfish, salmon, halibut, cod)

TOMATO CHUTNEY
½	cup cider vinegar
¼	cup sugar
1	pint cherry tomatoes, halved
1	medium-size onion, finely chopped
1–1½	tablespoons finely chopped, seeded jalapeño pepper (1–2 jalapeños)
1	tablespoon peeled, grated fresh ginger
2	cloves garlic, finely chopped
¼	teaspoon salt

SHARK
2	tablespoons fresh lime juice (2 limes)
1¼	pounds shark steaks

1. Prepare Chutney: Combine vinegar and sugar in medium-size nonaluminum saucepan. Bring to boiling, stirring to dissolve sugar. Boil 2 minutes. Add tomatoes, onion, jalapeño pepper, ginger, garlic and salt. Boil gently, stirring occasionally, for 1 hour, or until most of the liquid has cooked off. (Remaining liquid will be absorbed upon standing.) Cool to room temperature. Refrigerate in covered container for up to 1 month.

2. Prepare Shark: Pour lime juice into glass or enamel dish just large enough to hold fish in single layer. Place fish in dish; turn fish over to coat. Refrigerate, covered, turning occasionally, for 30 minutes.

3. Preheat grill or broiler. Grill or broil fish about 4 inches from heat for 4 to 6 minutes on each side, depending on thickness, or until fish is opaque in center and begins to flake when touched with a fork. Cut into 4 equal portions if necessary.

5. To serve, spoon chutney over fish.

Makes 4 servings (2 cups chutney).

223 CALORIES PER SERVING (WITH ¼ CUP CHUTNEY): 30 G PROTEIN; 7 G FAT; 11 G CARBOHYDRATE; 182 MG SODIUM; 72 MG CHOLESTEROL.

Soy-Glazed Shark Steaks With Shiitake Mushrooms

(also good with halibut, swordfish, salmon, cod steaks)

For complementary accents to this classic Asian flavor combination of sweet, tart and salty, serve with short-grain brown rice and a bean sprout and radish salad seasoned with rice vinegar.

¼   cup orange juice
2   tablespoons reduced-sodium soy sauce
2   tablespoons honey
1¼   pounds shark steaks
2   teaspoons vegetable oil
¼   pound shiitake mushrooms, trimmed, halved or quartered if large, or chanterelle or oyster mushrooms
2   cloves garlic, finely chopped
2   scallions, trimmed and thinly sliced

1. Combine orange juice, soy sauce and honey in medium-size bowl. Add shark steaks. Refrigerate, covered, for at least 1 hour and up to 4 hours, turning occasionally. Transfer to broiler pan, reserving marinade. Preheat broiler.

2. Broil fish about 4 inches from heat for 4 to 6 minutes, without turning, depending on thickness, until browned on top and opaque in center. Cut into 4 equal portions if necessary. Remove to serving plate; cover and keep warm.

3. Meanwhile, heat oil in medium-size nonstick skillet over medium-high heat. Add mushrooms; sauté 3 minutes. Add garlic; sauté 1 minute longer. Remove to plate with fish.

4. Add reserved marinade to same skillet. Gently boil 3 minutes, or until marinade is syrupy.

5. To serve, pour reduced marinade over fish and mushrooms. Garnish with scallions.

Makes 4 servings.

260 CALORIES PER SERVING: 31 G PROTEIN; 9 G FAT; 13 G CARBOHYDRATE; 361 MG SODIUM; 72 MG CHOLESTEROL.

Shrimp

THESE SALTWATER SHELLFISH are available fresh and quick-frozen, both cooked and raw, and occasionally you will find them with the heads still intact. Size varies from jumbo (21 to 25 per pound), extra-large (26 to 30 per pound), large (31 to 39 per pound), medium-large (36 to 40 per pound) and medium (41 to 50 per pound). Cook with or without the shells by any method, but be careful not to overcook or the shrimp will toughen.

Steamed Shrimp and Okra

(also good with crab, crawfish, monkfish, scallops)

This dish is great for company because it's simple to make, pretty to look at and light yet satisfying to eat. Serve over the Tomato Rice with a crisp green salad, a loaf of crusty bread and a bottle of dry white wine. *(See photograph on the back cover.)*

TOMATO RICE

1½	cups water
1	cup long-grain white rice
1	cup chopped, cored fresh tomatoes
¼	teaspoon salt
	Pinch ground hot red pepper (cayenne), or more to taste

SHRIMP AND OKRA

1	pound fresh or thawed frozen okra, halved crosswise
2	tablespoons fresh thyme leaves or 2 teaspoons dried
½	teaspoon celery seeds, crushed
½	teaspoon salt
¼	teaspoon ground hot red pepper (cayenne)
2	lemons, thinly sliced
1¼	pounds large shrimp, shelled and deveined (¾ pound cleaned)
¼	cup thinly sliced scallions

1. Prepare Tomato Rice: Combine water, rice, tomatoes, salt and hot red pepper in medium-size saucepan. Bring to boiling over medium heat. Lower heat; cover and simmer 20 minutes. Remove from heat. Let stand, covered, 10 minutes before serving.

2. Prepare Shrimp and Okra: Place okra on steamer rack over 1 to 2 inches of boiling water in large saucepot or kettle. Sprinkle evenly with 1 tablespoon fresh thyme (1 teaspoon dried), ¼ teaspoon celery seeds, ¼ teaspoon salt and ⅛ teaspoon hot red pepper. Cover with half the lemon slices. Top with shrimp. Sprinkle with remaining thyme, celery seeds, salt and pepper. Cover with remaining lemon slices. Cover pot.

3. Steam 8 to 10 minutes, or until okra is tender and shrimp is opaque. Serve at once over hot Tomato Rice. Sprinkle with scallions.

Makes 4 servings.

284 CALORIES PER SERVING: 20 G PROTEIN; I G FAT; 48 G CARBOHYDRATE; 563 MG SODIUM; I3I MG CHOLESTEROL.

Stir-Fried Shrimp With Sugar Snap Peas and Baby Corn

(also good with crab, lobster, monkfish)

To prevent foods from sticking, heat the wok for 1 minute before adding oil, then heat the oil before adding the sugar snaps. Serve this colorful combination with plain brown rice, or try it with aromatic basmati, Texmati or jasmine rice.

1	pound shrimp, peeled and deveined (12 ounces cleaned)
3	tablespoons reduced-sodium soy sauce
2	tablespoons rice-wine vinegar
½	teaspoon sesame oil
¼	teaspoon crushed red pepper flakes
2	teaspoons vegetable oil
2	scallions, trimmed, halved lengthwise and cut into 2-inch lengths
½	pound fresh sugar snap peas, trimmed, or 1 package (8 ounces) frozen, thawed
1	can (15 ounces) Oriental-style baby corn, drained, or ⅓ cup canned sliced water chestnuts, rinsed and drained

1. Combine shrimp, soy sauce, vinegar, sesame oil and red pepper flakes in large bowl; toss to coat. Refrigerate for 30 minutes, stirring occasionally.

2. Heat wok over medium-high heat. Add vegetable oil; heat. Add scallions; stir-fry 1 minute. Add sugar snaps; stir-fry 2 minutes. With slotted spoon, remove shrimp from marinade to wok; reserve marinade. Stir-fry 2 minutes longer. Add baby corn or water chestnuts and reserved marinade. Cook, stirring often, for 2 minutes, until bubbly and heated through. Serve at once.

Makes 4 servings.

193 CALORIES PER SERVING: 19 G PROTEIN; 4 G FAT; 23 G CARBOHYDRATE; 776 MG SODIUM; 131 MG CHOLESTEROL.

Marinate these shrimp no longer than 20 to 30 minutes or they may become spongy. Serve hot off the grill, or make up to a day ahead, refrigerate and serve cold with an Asian-stlye salad or a plain green salad.

Grilled Ginger Shrimp

(also good with sea scallops)

2   pounds extra-large or jumbo shrimp, shelled, with tails left on, deveined
2   tablespoons fresh lime juice (from 1 lime)
2   tablespoons reduced-sodium soy sauce
2   cloves garlic, crushed through a press
1   tablespoon peeled, grated fresh ginger
1   tablespoon vegetable oil
2   tablespoons finely chopped fresh cilantro or parsley (optional)

1. Combine lime juice, soy sauce, garlic, ginger and oil in large bowl. Add shrimp; toss to coat. Refrigerate, covered, 20 to 30 minutes.

2. Place shrimp in oiled grill basket or thread on skewers. (If using wooden skewers, soak skewers in water for 1 hour before using.) Preheat grill or broiler.

3. Grill or broil about 4 inches from heat for 2 to 3 minutes per side, turning once, or until shrimp are browned and just opaque in center. Sprinkle with cilantro or parsley, if using. Serve at once or refrigerate in covered container until ready to serve.

Makes 12 appetizer servings or 6 main-dish servings.

63 CALORIES PER APPETIZER SERVING: 11 G PROTEIN; 2 G FAT; 1 G CARBOHYDRATE; 196 MG SODIUM; 99 MG CHOLESTEROL.

126 CALORIES PER MAIN-DISH SERVING: 22 G PROTEIN; 3 G FAT; 1 G CARBOHYDRATE; 391 MG SODIUM; 197 MG CHOLESTEROL.

Snapper

SEVENTEEN SPECIES of snapper inhabit the waters of North America, with the popular red snapper accounting for most of the food fishing in the Gulf of Mexico. Yellowtail snapper ranges the Atlantic coast from Maine to the Gulf. The fish is sold whole—some species grow up to 3 feet long—or more often in fillets. Lean, sweet snapper fillets can be cooked by most any method. Often, the less flavorful and cheaper Pacific rockfish is sold, skinned, in place of the snapper—so know your source.

Red Snapper in Packets With Mango and Mint

(also good with cod, haddock, halibut, tilefish, grouper, tilapia, bluefish, swordfish, tuna, salmon)

A neat way to cook since both fish and side dish are steamed together in the same foil packet. Be sure to adjust cooking time whether using fillets or steaks. Serve with rice or a rutabaga puree or squash puree.

4	red snapper fillets (about 5 ounces each)
1	tomato, cored, seeded and chopped
1	small mango, pitted, skin removed and flesh chopped (about 1½ cups)
1	small red onion, chopped
2	tablespoons chopped fresh mint or 2 teaspoons dried
	Juice of 1 lime
½	teaspoon salt
½	teaspoon freshly ground black pepper

1. Preheat oven to 450 degrees F with baking sheet in oven.

2. Cut four 18 x 12-inch rectangles from heavy-duty aluminum foil. Place fillet in center of each piece of foil. Scatter tomato, mango, onion, mint, lime juice, salt and pepper over each fillet, dividing equally. Bring 2 long sides of foil up and over fish; fold edges over together twice. Fold short ends over twice to form tightly sealed packets.

3. Place foil packets on preheated baking sheet. Bake for 10 to 15 minutes, depending on thickness of fillets or steaks, or until fish is opaque in center and begins to flake when touched with fork. To check for doneness, carefully unwrap one packet.

4. To serve, carefully cut open each packet and place on plate, or let each diner open his or her own.

Makes 4 servings.

193 CALORIES PER SERVING: 30 G PROTEIN; 2 G FAT; 13 G CARBOHYDRATE; 334 MG SODIUM; 52 MG CHOLESTEROL.

Red Snapper With Soy and Ginger

(also good with cod, haddock, halibut, tilefish, grouper, tilapia, bluefish, tuna)

Adjust the heat in this dish by varying the amount of crushed red pepper flakes and fresh ginger, which is much more piquant than its dried, ground counterpart. Serve with steamed sugar snap peas and patty-pan squash, and sliced tomatoes dressed with balsamic vinegar and snipped fresh chives or, for an Asian touch, with wonton dumplings filled with vegetables.

½	cup reduced-sodium soy sauce
¼	cup dry sherry or dry vermouth
1	tablespoon peeled, grated fresh ginger
1	teaspoon Worcestershire sauce
½	teaspoon sesame oil
2	tablespoons chopped scallion
2	cloves garlic, crushed through a press
½	teaspoon crushed red pepper flakes
1¼	pounds red snapper fillets

1. Combine soy sauce, sherry or vermouth, ginger, Worcestershire, sesame oil, scallion, garlic and red pepper flakes in glass or enamel dish just large enough to hold fillets in single layer. Add fish to dish; turn to coat. Refrigerate, covered, turning occasionally, 30 to 60 minutes.

2. Preheat oven to 425 degrees F. Spoon a little marinade into a baking dish and spread to cover bottom. Transfer fillets to dish. Spoon a little marinade over fish; discard remaining marinade.

3. Bake for 8 to 12 minutes, depending on thickness of fillets or steaks, or until fish is opaque in center and begins to flake when touched with fork. Cut into 4 equal portions if necessary.

Makes 4 servings.

173 CALORIES PER SERVING: 31 G PROTEIN; 2 G FAT; 3 G CARBOHYDRATE; 696 MG SODIUM; 52 MG CHOLESTEROL.

Swordfish

SWIMMING ALONG both coasts in North and South America, swordfish can grow up to 15 feet long and weigh in at more than 1,000 pounds, with the average at about 250 pounds. The meat, usually sold as steaks, is firm-textured, full-flavored and a little oily, with a slight sweetness. Swordfish takes well to strong marinades and is excellent for broiling, grilling or baking.

Swordfish With Tomato and Herbs

(also good with tuna, monkfish, bluefish, shark, mackerel, cod, haddock, halibut)

1¼	pounds swordfish steaks
3	tomatoes, cored, seeded and coarsely chopped
2	cloves garlic, chopped
1	tablespoon fresh lemon juice
1	tablespoon chopped fresh thyme leaves or 1 teaspoon dried
1	tablespoon fresh rosemary leaves or 1 teaspoon dried
¼	teaspoon salt
¼	teaspoon freshly ground black pepper

1. Preheat oven to 425 degrees F. Place swordfish in baking dish. Scatter tomatoes and garlic over top. Sprinkle with lemon juice, thyme, rosemary, salt and pepper.

2. Bake for 8 to 12 minutes, depending on thickness of fillets or steaks, or until fish is opaque in center and begins to flake when touched with fork. Cut into 4 equal portions if necessary.

Makes 4 servings.

197 CALORIES PER SERVING: 29 G PROTEIN; 6 G FAT; 6 G CARBOHYDRATE; 269 MG SODIUM; 56 MG CHOLESTEROL.

A quickly put-together combination of tomatoes and herbs that will accent practically any fish, whether fillet or steak. To balance the full-flavored swordfish, accompany it with roasted beets and tiny red potatoes. (See photograph on the following pages.)

Broiled Swordfish With Apricot-Mustard Glaze

(also good with tuna, shark, salmon, mackerel)

¼	cup apricot jam
1	tablespoon Dijon-style mustard
1¼	pounds swordfish steaks
4	red radishes, coarsely grated, or daikon (Oriental white radish)

1. Preheat broiler. Combine jam and mustard in small bowl. Spread half of glaze evenly over one side of steaks.

2. Broil about 4 inches from heat for 4 to 6 minutes per side, depending on thickness of steaks or fillets, or until fish is opaque in center and begins to flake when touched with fork. Spread steaks with remaining glaze after turning over. Cut into 4 equal portions if necessary.

3. To serve, garnish steaks with shredded radish.

Makes 4 servings.

231 CALORIES PER SERVING: 28 G PROTEIN; 6 G FAT; 14 G CARBOHYDRATE; 181 MG SODIUM; 56 MG CHOLESTEROL.

Broiled Swordfish With Pineapple-Melon Salsa

(also good with tuna, shark, cod, mackerel, haddock, halibut, tilapia, monkfish, tilefish)

This spicy-sweet salsa goes with practically any fish and can be refrigerated for up to 2 days; be sure to let the salsa come to room temperature for best flavor. In a pinch, substitute canned pineapple chunks packed in juice, drained and patted dry with paper toweling. Serve leftover salsa as a salad on its own, or spoon over baked chicken, hamburgers or grilled flank steak. Mix with egg salad for sandwiches.

PINEAPPLE-MELON SALSA
- ½   cantaloupe, seeded, rind removed and finely diced
- ½   small ripe pineapple, halved lengthwise, rind removed, cored and finely diced
- 4   scallions, trimmed and finely chopped
- 2   tablespoons finely chopped fresh cilantro or flat-leaf parsley
- 2   tablespoons cider vinegar
- ¼–½   teaspoon crushed red pepper flakes

- 1¼   pounds swordfish steaks
     Lime wedges

1. Prepare Salsa: Combine cantaloupe, pineapple, scallions, cilantro or parsley, vinegar and red pepper flakes in small bowl. Refrigerate, covered, for 3 hours or up to 2 days. Bring to room temperature before using. Preheat broiler.

2. Broil fish about 4 inches from heat for 4 to 6 minutes on each side, depending on thickness of steaks or fillets, or until fish is opaque in center and begins to flake when touched with fork. Cut into 4 equal portions if necessary.

3. Serve with salsa and lime wedges on the side.

Makes 4 servings (about 4 cups salsa).

188 CALORIES PER SERVING (WITH ¼ CUP SALSA): 28 G PROTEIN; 6 G FAT; 4 G CARBOHYDRATE; 129 MG SODIUM; 55 MG CHOLESTEROL.

Trout

THIRTY-NINE SPECIES of trout inhabit both fresh and salt waters of North America. Two of the most popular trout are brook and rainbow, the latter now being farm-raised. Rainbow trout can measure up to almost 4 feet and weigh a little more than 40 pounds. Sweet-flavored and somewhat oily, trout is sold whole or in fillets and can be baked, broiled, grilled, poached or sautéed.

Spicy Trout Fillets

(also good with flounder, sole, orange roughy, hake, pollock)

½	cup low-fat plain yogurt
1	tablespoon mango chutney, large pieces chopped
¼–½	cup all-purpose flour
¼	teaspoon ground cumin
¼	teaspoon ground cinnamon
¼	teaspoon ground turmeric
¾	cup buttermilk
1¼	pounds trout fillets
2	teaspoons vegetable oil

1. Combine yogurt and chutney in small bowl.

2. Combine flour, cumin, cinnamon and turmeric on plate. Pour buttermilk into shallow plate. Dip trout fillets into buttermilk, then in flour mixture to coat on both sides; shake off any excess flour.

3. Heat oil in large nonstick skillet over medium-high heat. Add fillets; cook until golden brown on both sides and cooked through, about 2 to 3 minutes per side. Cut into 4 equal portions if necessary.

4. To serve, spoon yogurt mixture next to fillets on plates.

Makes 4 servings.

251 CALORIES PER SERVING (WITH 1 TABLESPOON SAUCE): 32 G PROTEIN; 8 G FAT; 11 G CARBOHYDRATE; 97 MG SODIUM; 84 MG CHOLESTEROL.

Turmeric turns the fillets a pleasing yellow, and the yogurt-chutney sauce marries well with the aromatic spice coating. Serve with a steamed green vegetable and parsleyed white rice.

Baked Trout With Lemon Stuffing

(also good with small whole mackerel)

7	slices white or whole-grain bread, crusts removed, cut into 1-inch cubes
1	tablespoon vegetable oil
5	cloves garlic, finely chopped
	Grated zest from 4 lemons
¾	cup finely chopped fresh flat-leaf parsley
½	teaspoon salt
½	teaspoon freshly ground black pepper
2	tablespoons fresh lemon juice
4	whole trout (about 12 ounces each), cleaned and boned
¼	cup dry white wine

1. Preheat oven to 450 degrees F. Place bread cubes in single layer on baking sheet. Bake bread cubes, stirring occasionally, until toasted, about 4 minutes. Leave oven at 450 degrees F.

2. Heat oil in medium-size nonstick skillet. Add garlic and lemon zest; stir until garlic is fragrant, about 30 seconds. Add ½ cup parsley, ¼ teaspoon salt, ¼ teaspoon pepper and the bread cubes. Stir in lemon juice. Remove from heat.

3. Season fish with remaining ¼ teaspoon salt and ¼ teaspoon pepper. Stuff each fish with one-quarter of the stuffing. Arrange fish in single layer in lightly oiled baking dish just large enough to hold fish. Sprinkle with wine.

4. Bake for 5 minutes. Reduce oven temperature to 400 degrees F. Bake until fish is opaque in center and begins to flake when touched with fork, 15 to 20 minutes. Let stand 3 minutes before serving.

5. To serve, sprinkle fish with any skillet juices and the remaining ¼ cup chopped parsley.

Makes 4 servings.

309 CALORIES PER SERVING: 37 G PROTEIN; 10 G FAT; 15 G CARBOHYDRATE; 446 MG SODIUM; 95 MG CHOLESTEROL.

Tuna

BLUEFIN, BIGEYE, YELLOWFIN AND ALBACORE are the most popular tunas for eating. The bluefin can measure up to 10 feet and weigh as much as 1,500 pounds. Usually sold as steaks, fresh tuna is fatty, firm-textured and strong-flavored. Strong marinades or herb and spice combinations go well with tuna, and the favored cooking methods are broiling, grilling and sautéing.

Tuna With Black Pepper

(also good with swordfish, shark, salmon)

¼ cup fresh lemon juice (1 lemon)
¼ cup fresh lime juice (2 limes)
¼ teaspoon salt
1¼ pounds tuna steaks
1 tablespoon cracked black pepper
1 cup mango chutney, chopped

1. Combine lemon juice, lime juice and salt in glass or enamel dish just large enough to hold the fish in a single layer. Place fish in dish; turn to coat. Refrigerate, covered, turning fish over occasionally, for 30 to 60 minutes.

2. Remove fish from marinade. Coat both sides of fish evenly with pepper, pressing to make sure pepper sticks. Preheat broiler.

3. Broil about 4 inches from heat for 4 to 6 minutes per side, depending on thickness of fish, or until fish is opaque in center. Cut into 4 equal portions if necessary.

4. Serve with the chutney on the side.

Makes 4 servings.

389 CALORIES PER SERVING (WITH ¼ CUP CHUTNEY): 36 G PROTEIN; 8 G FAT; 42 G CARBOHYDRATE; 209 MG SODIUM; 59 MG CHOLESTEROL.

This is very peppery—a fish version of steak au poivre. Marinating and quick broiling keep the fish moist. Feel free to vary the amount of cracked pepper. For a sandwich variation, spread pieces of toasted sturdy bread with a little reduced-calorie mayonnaise; garnish with watercress and very thin slices of lemon. This is also excellent with Yogurt-Scallion Sauce (page 19).

Tuna Salad With Yogurt-Dill Dressing

(also good with salmon, swordfish)

Using fresh fish rather than canned makes all the difference, and leftover cooked fish works well. The salad may be prepared a day ahead and refrigerated. For a great sandwich filling, keep the pieces of tuna small, and heap the salad on toasted peasant bread spread with chilled Sun-Dried Tomato Sauce (page 25), then garnish with romaine.

TUNA
- ½   cup fresh lime juice (4 to 6 limes)
- ½   red onion, thinly sliced
- 2   cloves garlic, crushed through a press
- ¼   teaspoon salt
- ¼   teaspoon freshly ground black pepper
- 1¼   pounds tuna steaks, cut into 1-inch cubes

DRESSING
- ¼   cup low-fat plain yogurt
- ¼   cup reduced-calorie mayonnaise
- 1–2   tablespoons chopped fresh dill or 1 tablespoon dried
- ¼   teaspoon salt
-   Pinch freshly ground black pepper

- ½   7-ounce jar roasted red peppers, chopped
- 3   scallions, trimmed and chopped

1. Prepare Tuna: Combine lime juice, red onion, garlic, salt and pepper in medium-size bowl. Add tuna; stir to coat. Refrigerate, covered, 2 to 3 hours, stirring occasionally.

2. Meanwhile, prepare Dressing: Combine yogurt, mayonnaise, dill, salt and pepper to taste in small bowl. Refrigerate, covered.

3. Remove tuna from marinade; discard marinade.

4. Cook tuna in large nonstick skillet, covered, over low heat until opaque in center, about 10 minutes. Let cool.

5. Place tuna in serving bowl. Flake with fork. Add red peppers and scallions. Gently fold in dressing.

6. Serve immediately, or refrigerate, covered, for up to 2 days.

Makes 4 servings (about 4 cups).

298 CALORIES PER SERVING: 38 G PROTEIN; 12 G FAT; 9 G CARBOHYDRATE; 340 MG SODIUM; 65 MG CHOLESTEROL.

Index